Plenty of Fish:

How To Hook The Client Who Needs Your Services

Chapter One

"You can't just place a few "Buy" buttons on your website and expect your visitors to buy." - Neil Patel

Picture this: you're walking in the mall and you stop at every single store. You eat at every single restaurant and sign up for every single promotional deal. That never happens, right? Do you know why that never happens? Because like the old saying goes: everything ain't for everybody.

Each store is marketed towards a specific customer. Forever 21 is for young adults so you'll never see an ederly man or woman shopping for themselves. Bunna Cafe is a restaurant for vegans so you'll probably never catch me there! But that's okay because they'll never market to me in the first place; therefore, it'll never cross my mind. I said all of this to say: the first step is knowing who you want to market to.

Chapter Two

"The best marketing doesn't feel like marketing." - Tom Fishburne

It's important that you don't get caught up in "how" to market. You want to build an organic relationship with your target audience. Here's some important things to remember:
1. No one really likes salesy people.
2. Education is key. If you teach people WHY they need your service or product then they will buy it.
3. Every client is not a good one. You want to market to people who need you, want you and are like you.
4. Don't chase; attract. You can only achieve #3 by being yourself, being honest about your talents and focusing on your own business/customers.
5. Enjoy what you do. People are attracted to passion and realness. You can tell a fraud from a mile away.

Chapter Three

"Content is anything that adds value to the reader"s life." - Avinash Kaushik

Now that we've tackled the "how" in marketing, let's focus on WHAT to market. It's very easy to do a lot of research and figure out things like brand identity, algorithms, influence, etc. yet forget that you still have to create great content. You know who you want to market to but how will you get their attention? By adding VALUE.
Life moves very fast, especially on social media. You could have the next billion dollar company but if you don't know how to keep the attention on you then you'll remain a startup. What kind of things will you promote? Will you use videos? (You better!) Will you post inspirational quotes? Will you be personal? These are the things that you will have to decide. Sure, you know how to get clients to sit at your table but what will you feed them so that they don't get up and leave. Or worse, sit at your competion's table.

Chapter Four

"Content builds relationships. Relationships are built on trust. Trust drives revenue." - Andrew Davis

Remember I said no one likes salesy people? It's because no one trusts them. How can you sell me something when you haven't asked me what I need? How can you sell me something when you haven't told me why you created it in the first place? How can you sell me something when I don't know you? Sure, there are certain buyers who don't have to be emotionally invested to purchase. However, they rarely return because there's no loyalty. There's no loyalty because there's no relationship.

Hook your clients by creating content that adds value to their lives. Once you add value, they will damn near trust you with their life (or at least their hair, nails, or makeup). Once that happens, they'll always put money in your pocket.

Chapter Five

"Social media is about sociology and psychology more than technology" - Brian Solis

Fun fact: I have a B.S in Psychology. No, I don't read minds but I do read people. I study people's personalities and figure out the role I need to play to keep them around. Don't get me wrong, I'll always be myself. However, it's important that you learn people's personal languages so that you know how to communicate with them emotionally, mentally and verbally. I very rarely sell anything on social media. It's just not fun to be THAT person. I learn my followers then I build organic relationships with them. Honestly, some of them are like the best friends I've never met and I love that. If you look at social media marketing as a task instead of a tool, you will lose every time. If you look at your clients as clients instead of friends, you will lose every time. If you look at your business as a business instead of a service to help others, YOU WILL LOSE EVERY TIME.

POP QUIZ

What is the first step before hooking your target client?

A. Marketing to my target audience
B. Creating beautiful content
C. Figuring out who I want to market to
D. Brand Identity

Answer: C

POP QUIZ

What is the key to marketing?

A. A large social media following
B. Educating your clients
C. Videos
D. Collaborations

Answer: B

POP QUIZ

How will you get your target clients' attention?

A. Sending them freebies
B. Following them on social media
C. By adding value to their lives
D. By making funny videos

Answer: C

POP QUIZ

Relationships are built on _____.

A. Support
B. Patience
C. Happiness
D. Trust

Answer: D

POP QUIZ

What should you learn about people in order to communicate with them emotionally, mentally and verbally?

A. Personal languages
B. Life story
C. Business ideas
D. Favorite color

Answer: A

Chapter Six

"Sell-sell-sell sales methods simply do not work on social media." -Kim Garst

Social media was literally created for users to be social. You are expected to be social amongst the friends you don't get to see often, strangers, family and even the friends you talk to regularly. Sell-sell-sell sales methods don't work on social media because that's not why it was created. People are most interested in building a relationship with you because you're funny, cool, fly, real, smart, talented, etc. Sure, they might be proud that you own a business but they don't really care. Use social media to build relationships, not to sale. It is a lot harder to attract the clients you want when you're turning all of them off by pushing your products and services all of the time. Attract your clients by being approachable. They should never feel like they're beneath you.

Chapter Seven

"Our digital future is about enabling better productivity and decision making to enjoy a better quality of life." - Yacine Baroudi

Selling to any and every client is a bad decision. Bad decisions do not lead to a better quality of life. In fact, they do the complete opposite. As a business owner, it is important to do things that are productive to your well-being. Productivity is feeding those who are sitting at your corner of the table rather than trying to feed the entire table. Not only would that lead to feeling burned out but it leads to a lower ROI. You would have to consistently push out content and products in hopes that SOMEONE will bite. Why do that when you could learn who your ideal clientele is and cater to that small group of people? Make decisions that will protect you and your business.

Chapter Eight

"Good marketers see consumers as complete human beings with all the dimensions real people have." –Jonah Sachs

Do you know why this is hard for you sometimes? Because you forget that your clients are human beings with regular human needs. Put yourself in their shoes. What would YOU want? What would make YOU happy? What would make YOU want to buy? Now, what is the difference between you and your target audience? Would you buy from a company with an ugly website or without one at all? Would you buy from a company that posts once every two months? Would you buy from a company that discrminates against marginalized groups? Would you buy from a company that doesn't have good customer service? As a business owner, you are often the client and the owner and it's important that you know how to look through the lens' of both roles.

Chapter Nine

"The consumer is not a moron; she is your wife." –David Ogilvy

As the saying goes, happy wife happy life. It is your job to love, respect, cherish and appreciate your wife. How can you treat your consumer like your wife, you ask? Show appreciation through sales and discounts. Show that you care by educating them on your service and why they need to make it a part of their lives. Show respect by providing extraordinary customer service. If your wife is unhappy, you will be unhappy because she can only treat you well when you're treating her well. From now on, forget the "client" mentality because it's making you treat them like one. These are people you've built relationships with! Don't take it for granted because you're not the only nor the best brand in the game. Protect your clients because you're protecting your business.

Chapter Ten

"People don't buy what you do, they buy why you do it." – Simon Sinek

Here's the honest truth: you're not that popping. Even if you are, there's 1000+ more of you in the same lane. People are drawn to the why. They are drawn to people that either remind them of themselves or inspire them. The best way to hook the client who needs you is by sharing your story and letting them know you're just like them. You need what they need. You want what they want. You've struggled with what they're struggling with. You overcame what they're going through. You believe what they believe. You miss Barack Obama too. You STAN Beyoncé as well. You used to be a waitress and a full-time student when you first started just like them. The client who needs you is the one who is just like you. How will you find them if you're not revealing who you are to anyone? It's never "just business" because there's too many options to choose from. Hook your ideal client by selling the "why" instead of the product.

POP QUIZ

Attract your clients by being _____.

A. Available
B. Approachable
C. Funny
D. Nice

Answer: B

POP QUIZ

_____ decision-making leads to a better quality of life.

A. Bad
B. Inconsistent
C. Unreliable
D. Good

Answer: D

POP QUIZ

As a business owner, you are often the _____ and the owner.

A. Friend
B. Boss
C. Client
D. Influencer

Answer: C

POP QUIZ

Happy wife, happy _____.

A. Life
B. Relationship
C. Family
D. Business

Answer: A

POP QUIZ

What are people drawn to?

A. Love
B. The why
C. Good jokes
D. Good content

Answer: B

– Juicee

Meetjuicee.com

@Meetjuicee
Twitter/IG/FB